The Jesus Prayer

The Jesus Prayer

Simon Barrington-Ward

The Bible Reading Fellowship
OPENING THE BIBLE

Text copyright © 1996 Simon Barrington-Ward
Illustrations copyright © 1996 Sister Teresa Margaret CHN

The author asserts the moral right to be
identified as the author of this work.

Published by
The Bible Reading Fellowship
Peter's Way, Sandy Lane West
Oxford OX4 5HG
ISBN 0 7459 3509 5

First edition 1996
10 9 8 7 6 5 4 3 2 1

Acknowledgements
Unless otherwise stated, scripture is taken
from the New Revised Standard Version of
the Bible, copyright © 1989 by the Division of
Christian Education of the National Council
of the Churches of Christ in the USA.

Revised Standard Version of the Bible (RSV),
copyright © 1946, 1952, 1971 by the Division
of Christian Education of the National
Council of the Churches of Christ in the USA.

A catalogue record for this book is
available from the British Library

Printed and bound in Great Britain
by Cox & Wyman Ltd, Reading, Berkshire

Contents

LORD JESUS CHRIST SON OF GOD HAVE MERCY ON ME

1

A first encounter with the Jesus Prayer

I came across the Jesus Prayer at a time when I was travelling in different parts of the world for the Church Missionary Society. It was those travels that made me hunger for a better way of praying, a way that would be more adequate to all that I was then encountering in Africa and Asia. Even on my return to this country I was becoming more aware than ever before of deep currents flowing in our own society.

Sometimes I could sense, underlying so many casual meetings and conversations across the globe, so many glimpses of the way people were living and striving and suffering—glimpses snatched even as I cycled into London, even around our offices in Waterloo—some kind of universal struggle. There seemed to be so many contradictions at every level in my life and in the whole of human society. There seemed to be, underlying everything, some kind of vast, inchoate yearning, which I could also feel, more and more of the time, in my own heart, and which seemed to be increasingly present in everything I was trying to do.

Gradually it focused on a longing for a real deepening of prayer—and of the whole of my 'life in Christ'. I was thirsting for something that was more universal, deeper, wider than my previous attempts at prayer. I was thirsting for a way of praying that genuinely embraced all the people and situations that still cried out to me when I paused for a moment, and yet at the same time came to grips more realistically with the frustrations and longings of my own divided nature.

One day a friend took me down to a Russian Orthodox monastery in Essex. It was just a small monastery, with both monks and sisters. This happened some years ago. Before that I had never had very much to do with the Orthodox Church.

As soon as we arrived we both went straight into the chapel, because the community and their guests were starting their evening Office. I imagined it was going to be like the Offices in most monasteries in the West, with some kind of traditional form like that of our own morning and evening prayer, which, after all, came out of the monastic tradition.

But instead they had something quite different. There was just one voice leading what has long been called 'the Jesus Prayer'—a woman's voice—and the others were praying it silently with her. We stood there in the darkened chapel, with all the ikons and screens around, and little lights burning. I was conscious of the shapes of the brothers and sisters around me, and of their faces. Faces as striking as that of Father Sophrony, a remarkable bearded countenance with a great quality of shrewdness and humour and also radiance about it, absorbed in the gentle flow of the prayer.

It was as if the faces of the brothers and sisters around me were somehow merging into the faces on the ikons all round on the walls—and I was conscious of how very easily you could find yourself one with them as the generations slipped back and back.

There was an ikon of St Silouan, the person from whom Father Sophrony had learned about the Jesus Prayer. I had seen Silouan's face in a photograph on the back of Father Sophrony's book about him; and now, there he was, in an ikon—which Father Sophrony told me later was a much better likeness of him than the photograph. The photograph was too sombre with his heavy eyebrows, dark gaze and massive beard dominating. The ikon showed the real lightness and the gleam of response which were also always there.

Then through the rows of smaller ikons we went back to the next generation, and back through the years to St Seraphim of Sarov with his white hair and beard and his white robe, bowed with frailty, but shining and alive with joy and risen life, and to all the great Russian saints before him, and before them reaching back to the Byzantine and Eastern Fathers and Mothers, and to the Desert Saints. And, at the heart of all, the Apostles—and John the Baptist, after whom the monastery was named. To the Evangelists, to St John and to the Virgin Mary and to the whole gospel story. Beyond us and over us was the Last Supper and above us the vision of God in heaven. It all seemed of a piece, as if we were all going forward together in this one great community in time and space and eternity.

That was the setting in which I first met the Jesus Prayer. And that whole setting was very important, because the prayer was already being said when we went into the chapel. The Sister who was leading it spoke the Jesus Prayer for quite a time. The prayer was in English, because all their liturgy is in English. Then a man took over. And they simply prayed the prayer:

'Lord Jesus Christ, Son of God, have mercy on me.'

There was a pause. And then the prayer was repeated. We were lifted up into the steady wing-beat of the prayer. As we settled into it and began to be drawn into it, we felt the whole focus of the whole community and of our own beings.

Our mind could wander—and we could even go to sleep. Yet all the time the prayer was going on, and we were part of it. The constant re-emphasis of the words 'Lord Jesus Christ' kept on recalling us to the presence. And the constant movement of the prayer, 'Have mercy on me', was something that immediately began to grasp me very deeply. After I came out of the chapel, the prayer was still praying itself inside me for many hours.

Afterwards I talked with Father Sophrony, and from that first occasion on we talked many times. He became a helper to me and a spiritual guide. He has since slipped through the veil—which in his presence always seemed so thin—that separates us still from that radiant host on the chapel wall. But, like the rest, he is still close to us. His shrewd twinkling gaze still looks across at me from a photograph on my study wall, peering quizzically across at me as he always did, as if he were humorously and affectionately aware of all one's evasions and yet always ready to guide one beyond them. And in this prayer particularly, I think we need that sort of help.

2

The corporate nature of the prayer

That community setting brought home to us the need for the prayer to be set within the corporate. We may be on our own when we are praying it, but we need to realize that we are praying it as part of the Christian community.

Many people have tried to do it on their own. There were *Franny and Zooey*, in J.D. Salinger's book, popular in the sixties, who picked up that widely read 'little pea green book' *The Way of a Pilgrim*, the 'travel notes' of a wandering spiritual seeker in nineteenth-century Russia, translated by R.M. French and published in Britain in 1930. The young hippy-like characters in Salinger's book tried the prayer described in the book as a kind of mantra, but not surprisingly without much success. And before he died Arnold Toybee tried desperately hard to pray the Jesus Prayer, but he couldn't find anything in it and it didn't seem to make any sort of sense. Again the reason is clear. This prayer can't really be extracted from the whole setting of faith and worship and participation in the life of the Church of which it is necessarily only a part.

When I entered that chapel I had already read and enjoyed *The Way of a Pilgrim* as some kind of an exotic story out of another age and culture, and had been attracted by it. But like so many Westerners, I simply hadn't realized how important the intensely *corporate* setting was in which I happened to be led into actually praying the Jesus Prayer myself.

But in fact the actual corporate recitation of the prayer was also quite unusual. Even in the Orthodox Church it is rare to find this prayer, essentially monastic though it is, prayed in that way. I am so grateful for having been introduced to the prayer in this setting. It rooted me in the knowledge that this, above all, is a prayer of the *Church*. It is thus a prayer that is all the time linking us with the whole community, past and present, and drawing us into the worship of those on earth and in heaven.

3

Trinitarian prayer

By the same token this is then seen to be also a pro-foundly trinitarian prayer. The Spirit is praying the prayer within us, and as we enter into those repeated words we become aware that the movement of the prayer is already taking place before we enter upon it and after we go out from it.

Someone said once that prayer is not getting on the telephone on a faulty line and struggling to get through to God. It is far more like stepping into a boat. Or we could think of it as plunging into the river ourselves, and being carried along and swim-ming in a current that is already moving. I believe it is very important to realize that. Indeed when that truth came home to me it made an enormous differ-ence to the way I was able to pray.

The Spirit is praying the prayer within us and amongst us. Without being enabled by the Spirit, St Paul told us, no one can say that Jesus is Lord (1 Corinthians 12:3). The Spirit bears witness with our spirit that we are children of God and indeed 'groans within us' helping us to cry, 'Have mercy on us', and leading us to the Son: 'Lord Jesus Christ, Son of God...'. There was a very strong and powerful emphasis on the word 'Son', and what gradually came home to me was that to say 'Son of God' was like saying 'Love of God'. And I found that I was also being drawn into the Father by praying to the Son 'in the Spirit'. So it is a totally trinitarian prayer.

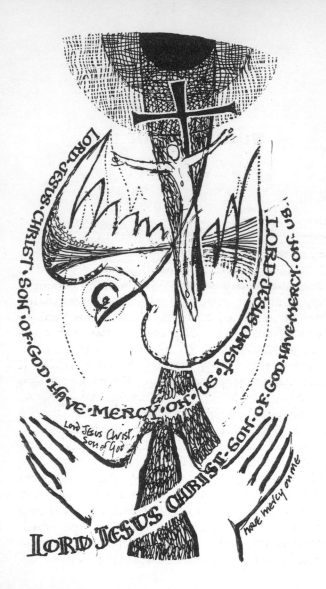

LORD JESUS CHRIST·SON·OF·GOD·HAVE·MERCY·ON·US·LORD·JESUS CHRIST·SON·OF·GOD·HAVE·MERCY·ON·US·

Lord Jesus Christ, Son of God

Have mercy on me

LORD JESUS CHRIST·SON·OF·GOD·HAVE·MERCY·ON·ME

14

4

The prayer of the whole creation: now and not yet (Romans 8)

There is also a sense in which the prayer links us with the whole of creation. I discovered this when I began to read about it. There was an excellent library at the monastery, and a bookshop, and I started to read while I was there and then I went on reading. I dipped into an anthology called the *Philokalia* (the 'love of [spiritual] beauty'), a marvellous book of extracts from writers about the Jesus Prayer through the ages. This anthology was compiled in the eighteenth century by two Russian Orthodox writers. It goes right the way back through the whole Russian and Eastern tradition of this kind of praying from its beginnings in the time of persecution and in the desert, as it grew out of biblical beginnings.

When I began to read all these extracts on the prayer, I soon found out about the way in which it links us with the whole creation. Those who pray 'have mercy upon me' have always been given a strong awareness that the whole creation was also crying out with them. The Bible passage which expresses this most deeply is Romans 8, because there, in what is one of the fullest expressions of 'the gospel according to St Paul' there is a threefold 'groaning' described. First we are told that it is the groaning of the creation itself, 'groaning' in the 'travail' (AV) or the 'labour pains' (NRSV) of the new creation which has begun in Christ's incarnation, death and resurrection (Romans 8:19–22). Then, secondly, it is the groaning with which we ourselves 'groan inwardly' as we wait for our own final 'adoption' when we are fully drawn into Christ's risen life (Romans 8:23–25). Thirdly, and most amazingly, God himself, 'the Spirit' groans, pleading, interceding, on our behalf with 'groanings that cannot be uttered' (Romans 8:26–27). There is here portrayed a kind of passion of the Holy Spirit, God himself, suffering and yearning within us as we struggle in our weakness to pray.

In this whole chapter 8 of Paul's letter to the Romans there is a marvellous poise and balance between two things. We are there—in the presence, in the love: 'There is therefore now no condemnation...'. It is all complete, and joyful, and the Spirit within us is crying, 'Abba, Father'. Yet at the same time, alongside that, there is this overwhelming sense of longing and of 'not yet'. We are 'being killed all the day long; we are accounted as sheep to be slaughtered' a verse St Paul quotes from the Psalms (Psalm 44:22) which had often been applied to the Jewish martyrs for their faith. It is now applied to Christians who are persecuted, as it was later to be applied to those who in 'white martyrdom' as it was to be called, sought to sacrifice themselves for prayer and for the renewal of the Church as it seeks to prepare for the kingdom.

But then there is the triumphant holding together of these two things together by the end of the chapter:

'neither death, nor life, nor angels, nor rulers, nor things present, nor things to come, nor powers, nor height, nor depth, nor anything else in all creation, will be able to separate us from the love of God in Christ Jesus our Lord.'

This amazing equipoise or balance of grace in St Paul comes out in so many places. Most strongly of all in that chapter 8 of Romans, and also in Philippians chapter 4 where in prison, possibly near to the end of his life and mission, Paul can say that 'I am able to be abased and I am able to abound. I can do all things through him who strengthens me' (Philippians 4:10–13). He conveys so often this strong sense of having all things in Christ now, but also of not having them wholly as yet.

> *Not that I have already obtained this [the resurrection from the dead] or am already perfect; but I press on to make it my own, because Christ Jesus has made me his own.*
> **Philippians 3:12 (RSV)**

As I prayed the Jesus Prayer and read about it and studied it, I was led into a different and a deeper understanding of prayer which brought me a little closer to this 'balance' of St Paul's than I had been before. I began to realize that prayer in Christ is always adoration, resting, rejoicing, thanksgiving and worship. Above all, it is an awareness of being loved. And as we become more and more aware of being loved and accepted, we find ourselves being drawn into the whole joy of the creation and of the ultimate fulfilment of the creation, the 'Divine Comedy'.

Prayer is essentially an entering into that knowledge of the divine love holding us. It is an entering into being loved—and even while we are dirty, broken, battered and may feel unworthy, we are in reality being swept into this tremendous acceptance. I believe that this is the beginning and the end of prayer. Being grasped by this love. As we dwell in that love, and rest in it, we find ourselves rejoicing and giving thanks.

Of course we all have an instinctive sense—which you can't help having if you become aware of being in the presence of God—of being unclean, unholy, unready. And that feeling can rightly be painful. But, at this point, we invoke the name of Jesus: a name to which George Herbert using the form, 'Jesu,' wanted to give the meaning 'I ease you'; a name which for him expressed the love which bids us welcome and wants to make us at home and even to wait upon us, as Christ waited upon his disciples, washing their feet. As we invoke Jesus' name, we must let God's 'yes' to us in Christ overcome all our negative feelings and affirm us fundamentally.

The feeling of unworthiness is absolutely understandable. It is all part of a genuine yearning to be different, which we feel when we enter into God's presence. It is just like the feeling you have when you come into the presence of someone who loves you very much and who is a very wonderful person whom you greatly admire and respect. And that person is obviously so happy to see you. They are someone who knows you through and through, who clearly perceives all your flaws and your failings. You thus feel a double feeling. You rejoice as if you had never really known yourself before. You begin to believe that you really are of worth. And that is a good sensation. But yet at the same time you feel

'I'm not up to this'. In the end, you are both over-joyed at the sense of potential good which the encounter has given you and also filled with a longing to be different. You go out really wanting to be, and believing that you can be, more the person that you have been shown that you really are than you ever felt possible before. And this is what the sense of the presence of God in Christ can give us, a strong desire to become what we truly are.

It is as I have been through the exercise of the Jesus Prayer—and really only through this—that I have gradually seen more and more how totally this recognition of what we are, *and* of what we have in us to be, is held together within the recollection of God's loving presence in the words 'Lord Jesus Christ, Son of God…' and then the longing cry of the prayer: 'Have mercy on me…'. That cry is so much more than just grovelling over my sins. It is a longing for a transformation, both an inner and an outer transformation, a transformation within the microcosm of my own heart and the macrocosm of the universe.

This is why the prayer is caught up into the groaning of the whole creation. 'Have mercy on *me*…'—but I become the contact point, as it were, with all things. I become the point of contact with others, with all those for whom I am praying. I can put the name of other people there sometimes. 'Have mercy on him… on her… on them…' the person or the people who are in my prayer. Sometimes the monks and nuns at the monastery I went to would substitute at the end, for the normal second phrase of the prayer, almost as a kind of reminder that this had been implicit all the time, 'Have mercy upon us and upon our world…'.

19

20

What they were doing was bringing out the fact that it is the universal cry that is crying out through us—each one of us being just a little fragment of creation. It is the longing cry of the saints 'under the altar', calling out, 'How long? How long?' in Revelation (6:9). It is the longing for the fulfilment and the consummation of all things.

There are always these two aspects of prayer: the yearning and the rejoicing. The yearning is always within the rejoicing. And Christ himself holds these wonderfully together. He is the only point in any faith, or at any point in this world or beyond it, at which I have ever felt that these two realities—the 'now' and the 'not yet'—are so totally held together or ever could be, because of the cross and the resurrection.

The power of Christ's resurrection and the fellowship of his sufferings (Philippians 3:10) are even carried into the vision of God in heaven. When we are caught up into prayer we cannot escape into heaven on cloud nine, and forget the struggle of this world, because Christ is there in the midst of heaven, 'ever living to make intercession for us', and carrying our wounds into the very heart of the triune God.

What matters is this holding together of rejoicing and yearning. That is why I treasure a lithograph by Georges Rouault, that powerful French artist from the time between the wars who responded so sensitively to the sickness and subterfuge, the folly and pain of his society and depicted it so trenchantly. His *Head of Christ* hangs here in the chapel of the Bishop's House. It shows him wearing a heavy tangled crown of thorns pressed down upon his head, his eyes cast downward in a strange fusion of agony and serenity, strength and exhaustion. It is imprinted upon a square as if it were derived from a negative. Or as if it were indeed the impression of the features of the crucified Christ left on St Veronica's handkerchief. This paradoxically gives it a strange immediacy. The inscription which Rouault put under one such depiction of the crucified was 'Jesus will be in agony until the end of the world', a recognition perhaps of the truth that 'he ever lives to make intercession for us' (Hebrews 7:25).

To pray the Jesus Prayer is to enter into something of the sorrow and suffering of Christ. It is to share in Christ's longing to serve, and to bear something of the pain of the world. That is our task and our calling.

5

Prayer in a brief phrase: its biblical roots

In the Sermon on the Mount Jesus tells us not to use 'vain repetitions' (Matthew 6:7, AV) and not to imagine that we shall be heard simply because we go on and on, as it were. But there is all the difference in the world between a vain repetition and the repetition of the Jesus Prayer. There are times when we can only express some of our deepest feelings by repeating some very simple phrase, such as, 'I'm sorry, truly sorry' or, 'thank you so much' or even, 'I love you'. Short prayers which have been said to 'pierce heaven' are like this also. They express a response to God or an aspiration which is almost too deep for words.

What the phrases of the Jesus Prayer do is give the top of our mind something to be occupied with, so that the rest of the mind can be open to the deeper feeling that lies underneath. This is what those who have used the prayer have called putting the mind in the heart. The words occupy our surface being at the same time as they communicate with the depths of us.

I believe that is why many people find it so helpful to use beads when they pray. And the Orthodox have a knotted cord which they use in this kind of way. It can have a hundred knots on it, and the monks use one knot each time they say the Jesus Prayer once.

A Russian monk gave me one of these cords, and I started to use it. Then one day I was at an ecumenical gathering in Oxford where people had been studying the prayer under the guidance of one of the monks from the Essex monastery. We went up into the chapel, in which everything had been arranged by him, with candles and ikons. And he asked me if I would like to lead the prayer, because we had been talking about the way they do it at the monastery. I was staggered to be asked, but I said yes. I was really nervous—so much so that I felt I would hardly be able to speak.

Then he said quietly to me, 'Give them a hundred!' in a quite casual and confiding way. Suddenly I realized that I had the cord in my pocket. So I didn't have to worry about it. I simply held it in my hands and said the prayer aloud on each knot.

To use the cord like this helps to occupy your body in a similar way to that in which the prayer is occupying the fingers of your mind, as it were. Your fingers move on round the cord, and they keep taking the prayer on and on. And as this happens it becomes a rhythm, or a ritual.

You don't have to keep thinking about what you are saying, or how you are speaking or what you are thinking. You don't make an image or a picture. You just have a sense of the presence—like being with someone in the room sitting in the firelight or walking with someone you know well and love, in either case being silent, with no need to say anything. There is a sense of just being *with* each other, and of feeling completely at ease. Just being with each

25

other—and this deep sense of the other's presence. This is maintained by the repetition of the prayer.

The vain repetition which Jesus was telling us to shun and avoid means heaping up phrases. They don't have very much relation to reality, so as my words go up, my heart remains below. But the Jesus Prayer is much more a cry *from* the heart which is being expressed; more like 'I love you' being repeated, or somebody's name being repeated—and you are saying it to someone with whom you are in a very close relationship.

The publican's repetition of the words, 'God, be merciful to me, a sinner' was the only way he could express the deep sorrow that he felt. And Bartimaeus' cry, 'Jesus, Son of David, have mercy on me!' was the only way he could express his longing to be healed.

Deep, loving praise, or deep yearning, seem to find a perfect expression in a repeated phrase—like the reiteration of a phrase in a Psalm: 'Bless the Lord, O my soul' (Psalm 103); or, 'Hope in God for I shall yet praise him, my help and my God' (Psalms 42 and 43), or the reiterated refrain in King Solomon's prayer at the dedication of the first temple, 'Hear in heaven, your dwelling place, and when you hear forgive!' (1 Kings 8; 2 Chronicles 6). This last is one of the most memorable Old Testament examples of a repeated formula:

> *'But will God indeed dwell on the earth?*
> *Behold, heaven and the highest heaven*
> *cannot contain thee; how much less this*
> *house which I have built! Yet have regard to*
> *the prayer of thy servant and to his*
> *supplication, O Lord my God, hearkening to*

the cry and to the prayer which thy servant
prays before thee this day; that thy eyes may
be open night and day toward this house, the
place of which thou hast said, "My name
shall be there," that thou mayest hearken to
the prayer which thy servant offers toward
this place. And hearken thou to the
supplication of thy servant and of thy people
Israel, when they pray toward this place; yea,
hear thou in heaven thy dwelling place; and
when thou hearest, forgive.'

1 Kings 8:27–30 (RSV)

6

What the Desert Fathers took from the New Testament

There was a strong New Testament influence on the way of praying which came to be adopted quite possibly in the early Church and amongst those who endured persecution or martyrdom. It was most strikingly present amongst those who, in the late third and fourth centuries, in reaction against the increasing worldliness of the Church, withdrew to the desert to seek a more perfect discipleship, obedience to God, and purity of heart. For them as much as for the martyrs, from the start, the greatest need was to turn with one's whole being to seek the power and grace of God in the person of Jesus Christ. The stories of the disciples in the first three Gospels—which had been written partly to strengthen and encourage the persecuted Christian communities of the first century—came again to the aid of those who, two centuries later, found themselves in solitude in the wilderness, wrestling with the evil one.

What spoke particularly to the early hermits and monks, from St Antony onwards, was something more than that extraordinary quest for perfection which they shared with many of the philosophical wanderers and pilgrims of the ancient Greek world—Neoplatonist, Cynic or member of a mystery cult. They wanted to look to Jesus alone, and to seek a more complete discipleship, after the example of those who had been ready to lay down their lives for him. The prayers that inspired them from the Gospels were the short appeals out of desperation and out of helplessness, out of longing for healing, or out of profound repentance, sorrow for sin and humbling. These were prayers to which Jesus in the stories responded so immediately and transformingly. They would cite prayers such as the cry of the ten lepers in Luke (17:13), 'Jesus, Master, have mercy on us'; or the two blind men in Matthew (9:27), 'Have mercy on us, Son of David'; or the Syro-Phoenician woman, 'Have mercy on me, O Lord, Son of David.'

Later the determined prayer that paralleled these others—that of blind Bartimaeus sitting by the roadside, and refusing to be stopped by those who tried to silence him (Mark 10:46–52)—became an example of true persistence in prayer, the virtue which Jesus commended in the importunate widow who wins her way with the judge (Luke 18), or the friend who at night rouses his neighbour to give him bread for his guest (Luke 11:5–8).

> As [Jesus] approached Jericho, a blind man
> was sitting by the roadside begging. When
> he heard a crowd going by, he asked what
> was happening. They told him, 'Jesus of
> Nazareth is passing by.' Then he shouted,
> 'Jesus, Son of David, have mercy on me!'
> Those who were in front sternly ordered him
> to be quiet; but he shouted even more loudly,
> 'Son of David, have mercy on me!' Jesus
> stood still and ordered the man to be brought

> to him; and when he came near, he asked
> him, 'What do you want me to do for you?'
> He said, 'Lord, let me see again.' Jesus said
> to him, 'Receive your sight; your faith has
> saved you.' Immediately he regained his
> sight and followed him, glorifying God; and
> all the people, when they saw it, praised God.
>
> Luke 18:35–43 (NRSV)

Bartimaeus throws off his cloak when at last they tell him that he is being summoned, symbolizing perhaps his casting away anything that would hinder him in seeking Jesus' help. Having received his sight from Jesus, he followed him 'on the way', a phrase which clearly signified discipleship henceforth. He thus becomes a model of one seeking Jesus and being enabled both to see Jesus' true identity and to follow him.

But the supreme Lucan passage, which immediately follows that of the importunate widow, was one which was to come to be seen as a model of heartfelt penitence and of the prayer of genuine self abasement. Jesus commends this as being another way in which a short, simple and repeated prayer goes straight to the heart of God. This was the prayer of the publican in the temple who went down to his house justified, in contrast with the Pharisee. Here he uses a different word from those who, in the stories I have mentioned, cried to Jesus, in the word we know from our liturgies, *eleison*. He beats his breast, saying, '*hilastheti* to me, a sinner!' Literally it is 'be propitious' or almost 'make propitiation' for me. It would perhaps be fanciful to see a hint of the cross in a usage which would more commonly have meant in this form 'be gracious to me'. But that

appeal for an atoning grace is most certainly met fully in the cross. No wonder this prayer was later to have such an appeal to those seeking compunction and repentance as they struggled in solitude, and placing themselves, as it were, at the foot of the cross. The parable, placed alongside that of the widow and the judge would seem to follow our first theme of bold and importunate appeal with that of utter surrender and brokenness.

> He also told this parable to some who trusted
> in themselves that they were righteous and
> regarded others with contempt. 'Two men
> went up to the temple to pray, one a Pharisee
> and the other a tax collector. The Pharisee,
> standing by himself, was praying thus, "God,
> I thank you that I am not like other people:
> thieves, rogues, adulterers, or even like this
> tax collector. I fast twice a week; I give a
> tenth of all my income." But the tax collector,
> standing far off, would not even look up to
> heaven, but was beating his breast and
> saying, "God, be merciful to me, a sinner!" I
> tell you, this man went down to his home
> justified rather than the other; for all who
> exalt themselves will be humbled, but all who
> humble themselves will be exalted.'
>
> Luke 18:9–14 (NRSV)

The conventional prayer of the Pharisee points to a genuine danger in devout religious observance of a certain complacency setting in. G.B. Caird pointed to prayers from Rabbinic literature which seem to sound a little of the same note as the Pharisee's prayer in this story. There is the prayer from the

GOD B...

...IPUL TO ME

GOD BE MERCIFUL TO ME A SINNER

GOD BE MERCIFUL TO ME A SINNER

33

Jewish Prayer Book: 'Blessed art Thou, O Lord our God, King of the Universe, who hast not made me a Gentile... Blessed art Thou... who hast not made me a slave. Blessed art Thou... who hast not made me a woman...'

The publican went down to his house 'justified' because he had been prepared to humble himself, and all who humble themselves will be exalted. All that he had was his need for God's forgiveness. Like the penitent thief on the cross or the woman who wiped Jesus' feet with her hair, he had only a repeated request like a kind of deep sigh of the heart—like the groaning of the Spirit in Romans 8—to bring. He could only throw himself on God's mercy. Jesus depicts, and in his own person enacts, God's instant response: 'Anyone who comes to me I will never drive away' (John 6:37).

Such prayers as that prayer of the publican express the profound and universal yearning in the hearts of so many, the cry of the very wounded creation itself. All that he could do in the face of God and in the knowledge of his own helpless failure was to repeat his prayer, and into those repeated words flowed the whole stream of his innermost life, all that was in him. Beside such a torrent, the complacent formula of the other man's prayer was swept aside. Small wonder that this heart-cry of the publican was to become a model for those who later sought wholeheartedly to follow Jesus in the desert. As they went apart to search for him and, seeking to draw closer, became aware of their immense distance from him, they too could be thrown back on such a brief, repeated phrase directing all the desires of their heart, all their aspiration towards the One who alone could save them.

In the Sayings (*Apothegmata*) of the Desert Fathers of the fourth and fifth centuries in Egypt and Syria and Palestine, there is evidence of the use of a whole variety of such brief repeated prayers, often echoing the Gospels, and addressed either to 'God', 'Son of God', 'Lord', or 'Jesus'. The two appeals most common might be either 'have mercy' (*eleison*) or 'help' (*boethai*), although there was also, of course, again from the Gospels, 'save me!'—an echo sometimes of Peter sinking in the waves: *sozon me!* St Antony, the model of all such hermits who became the inspiration of the Church, once persecution and martyrdom had ended, repeatedly prayed, 'How can I be saved?' He saw in the repetition of this kind of short prayer an opportunity to occupy the surface of your mind while you turn your whole attention to the presence of God, when he said that this was 'perfect prayer'. 'The prayer is not perfect,' he remarked, 'in which the monk is conscious of himself or of the fact that he is praying.'

So many of these anchorites and solitaries spoke of having a 'secret prayer' not lightly to be spoken of, a phrase or a scripture verse such as the prayer of Bartimaeus or of the tax collector. These were at the very heart of their *politeia* or 'hidden' way of life. They were expressions of that 'joyful mourning' (*penthos*), recollection (memory, *mnemne*) of God in the heart, or secret meditation (*meleta*). This word often meant speaking a verse or saying it repeatedly aloud and savouring it, and the monks were known to have been overheard through their doors, saying or even singing these in their cells.

This practice was described by John Cassian (360–435) who himself went round visiting so many of these people of prayer, seeking to learn from them before settling in his own hermitage in the West and writing his *Institutes*. By that time he had adopted for his own *meleta* the verse, 'O God, make haste to help me: O God, make speed to save me.' The very use of that phrase, familiar from the Prayer Book, serves to remind us how much our liturgies were shaped by the monks, and their liturgies in turn by the earliest desert tradition. For John Cassian this kind of 'meditation' was a powerful means of keeping alive in us 'a continual memory of God and maintaining ceaseless prayer'.

Already many of these early pioneers of prayer refer to St Paul's command that we should 'pray without ceasing' (1 Thessalonians 5:17), which was to become a theme of the whole quest for the secret of prayer from those days up until recent times in the Eastern Church and in Russia. Cassian would rise in the night at intervals to continue his rapt repetition of this verse as it lifted his mind and heart into one continuous prayer. It was this above all that he had learnt from his survey of the solitaries in the deserts of Egypt and Palestine. For him it became the secret of living a life continuously interwoven with the life of God.

7

The emergence of the distinctive nature of the Jesus Prayer

There were, of course, strong influences at work on the early history of this prayer which were very far from biblical. The whole atmosphere of thought and spirituality within which early Christianity developed was shaped by influences from the East. The culture of the Roman Empire, especially in its Eastern half, was dominated by a so-called Hellenism and Platonism which itself had some affinities with Indian ways of thinking and praying. Already in the second century, Christian thinkers, supremely Origen, were developing systems, pictures of the world, which emphasized spirit and 'intellect' and tended to see matter and the material world as evil. The present created order, and within it the human body, had come into being as a result of the 'Fall' and were a result of sin. Prayer was the way in which we attained to a spiritual state through which in the end we would return, through union with a spiritualized Christ, to life in God. This kind of teaching appealed to intellectually and mystically minded Greeks who even joined the monastic movement as a result.

Evagrius of Pontus (346–399) was one of the solitaries who developed Origen's teaching to give an interpretative framework to the life and prayer of monks, nuns and hermits. His writing the *Gnostic Centuries* had a powerful effect on the spirituality of those who prayed in desert cells and monasteries. Indeed much of his practical and psychological teaching about the nature of human passions and how to overcome them entered into the whole monastic tradition and was repeated in all the writings of many later great spiritual teachers of this movement in the Eastern Church.

Thankfully another influence was at work. There was a large body of anonymous 'homilies' attributed (wrongly) to a contemporary of Evagrius called Macarius. These took their interpretation of prayer from the experience of the desert solitaries who espoused the kind of New Testament prayers I have described. There could be a danger in Evagrius' more 'Easternized' teaching of a short repeated prayer becoming something of a mantra leading into a some kind of rather abstract spirituality and striving to transcend the body and the material world altogether.

But for the *'Macarian' Homilies* the focus of prayer was much more definitely on the *incarnate* Christ. It was a prayer not just of the spiritualized 'mind' but of the *heart*. As through repentance and forgiveness we come into communion with Jesus Christ, crucified and risen, we begin to arrive at the transformation of our whole being, body and soul, together with all those who share the same quest.

Through the practice of prayer, through an ascetic discipline and through the eucharist, we are given the strength and the assurance to overcome the power of evil with which we struggle in the 'heart', the centre of our being, until body and soul are redeemed and united with God. This is the concrete, personal practice of ceaseless prayer as the Desert Fathers knew it. It is both corporate and physical as well as spiritual. St Antony, the great prototype of such a way of life, is described by his biographer, St Athanasius, as possessing all his faculties and his body complete in every part, even when he was frail and old, as one already moving towards ultimate bodily resurrection.

Such was the distinctive approach to prayer, different in its key features from that of Evagrius, which was taken up into the work of the writers of the fifth century—people such as Bishop Diadochus of Photike in Greece, or his contemporary in Asia Minor, Nilus of Ancyra. These teachers of prayer gathered the Desert traditions into one, and, following the Macarian lead perhaps, focused more firmly and clearly than ever on the practice of the presence of Jesus and on growth into his *agape* (love).

They now spoke of 'ceaselessly calling on the name of the Lord Jesus' and of the 'ceaseless remembrance of His name'. 'You must take this alone for your meditation and constant occupation, renouncing your own will as you constantly seek healing and purity of heart'.

The sense of the intense importance of the name of every being was a strong feature of the ancient world, as it has been of all traditional cultures. It is a theme in the Bible itself. The name discloses the hidden nature and the distinctive power and quality of every being. When it is revealed it makes that being vulnerable and accessible. Look at the importance of giving names both to places, and to people, above all, in the Old Testament and the New, and of being called by your name. To invoke the name of a god or a spirit was to seek to relate to that divine being's special secret. For that divinity to reveal its name is for it to open its nature to the worshipper in a striking way. We recall Jacob wrestling with the angel, 'Tell me, I pray you, your name.' Thus when God at once conceals and reveals his name to Moses, in the mysterious announcement, 'I Am that I Am' or 'I will be that I will be', it is the foundation of a whole new relationship, a whole new discovery or rather self-revelation of the divine. The whole covenant is implicit in this moment of truth, in what is in some sense a mutual commitment between God and frail humanity, a moment of compassionate entrusting.

Even in modern times, for some, their discovery of God has been bound up with this amazing sense of an opening up of personal communion between God and ourselves. There was Pascal's encounter with the One who was 'the God of Abraham, Isaac and Jacob, not the God of the philosophers!' He kept the record of this astonishing experience of grace sewn in the lining of his coat until the day of his death. Father Sophrony's own moment of conversion had come through a disclosure of God in his great and overwhelming love, the God of Moses and of Jesus, the 'I Am' of the new covenant, in whom he found the truth far beyond his previous mystical illusions as they now seemed. He painted a great ikon in the refectory of the monastery to reflect the infinitely mysterious reality of the 'I Am', the *living* God.

The great emphasis on the name of Jesus in the New Testament reflects this whole theme. His name is his real nature and, like so many other names of significant people in the Bible, is revealed by God. 'You are to name him Jesus [Joshua or Jeshua, 'one who saves'], for he will save his people from their sins' (Matthew 1:21). And his name becomes integral to the new covenant, the new relationship with God which he brings (hence Matthew's reference to the prophecy in Isaiah 7: '"They shall name him Emmanuel", which means "God is with us."'). Christians become those who 'had his name and his Father's name written on their foreheads' (Revelation 14:1); those who are persecuted and hated 'for the name' who invite people to 'call upon the name' are 'baptized into the name'. They are to 'do all in the name of the Lord'. This is the name above all names which every tongue shall confess and before which every knee shall bow (Philippians 2:9–11). In St John's Gospel supremely, Jesus himself places this emphasis on the name. In prayer he tells the disciples that what they ask 'in my name' the Father will give to them (John 15:16; 16:23–24). In his name God will send them the Holy Spirit (John 14:26). He made known the 'name' of God to them (John 17:26). This is surely a reference to his saying to them, 'Whoever has seen me has seen the Father' (John 14:9). He has kept them in the Father's name which the Father has given him (John 17:12). The two names seem to be identified with each other here. 'That they might know you, the only true God, and Jesus Christ whom you have sent' (John 17:3). The name of Jesus becomes the very expression of the true nature, the infinite justice and mercy of God.

The sixth century saw an emphasis on not only short repeated prayer but on the name of Jesus as its object in several other key works of teaching, some taking the form of biography of people of prayer such as St Dositheos, an eager young man being urged as he lay dying by his spiritual guide to 'set his heart on fire with the continuous memory of the Lord Jesus'; or Abba Philemon, whose 'secret meditation' was revealed to be none other than 'Lord Jesus Christ, have mercy on me!' He claimed to have received this from Bishop Diadochus who had taught that we should repeat it in our minds 'soberly, with fear and trembling'. It was for him 'the prayer which no one could say but by the Holy Spirit' (1 Corinthians 12:3). It was the prayer he prescribed for beginners. Through this kind of prayer addressed to the Lord Jesus we were to sustain the habitual thought and memory of him. Philemon, who spoke, as many of the Fathers had done, of the importance of solitude and silence (*hesychia*), saw in the Jesus Prayer, above all, the means of concentrating and filling that silence with the 'memory of God'.

No wonder such a prayer was experienced as a way of prayer that could heal and reintegrate our consciousness divided by sin, cleanse us of our sickness and purify us, and restore us to that wholeness for which we were made. By the time the monks of Sinai were recording and transmitting the whole earlier Christian spiritual tradition, clearly the prayer invoking the name of Jesus had become an established strand in that tradition.

There was certainly no set form, nor indeed might the name of Jesus necessarily be specifically mentioned in the short prayers people used, but the recollection of his presence and quest for his help were never far off. The monastic picture of human beings at prayer is of those who stand as creatures before their maker, inwardly naked and needy. Those who petition God out of profound spiritual poverty, 'a beggar before the Lord of Heaven and earth,' in a state of repentance or mourning (*penthos*) humbling oneself and crying out like a beggar for help from the One who possesses infinite riches. In this state it was increasingly common to invoke the name of Jesus, and the cry of Bartimaeus or the prayer of the publican were echoed.

In the mid-seventh century, John Climacus in the great monastery of Sinai, in his great work *The Ladder of Paradise*, drew together all the elements of this classical desert spirituality. There was a strong flavour of Evagrius' austerity and tendency to despise the body in his asceticism. But in his teaching on prayer once again he emphasized the centrality of the person and name of Jesus which was an effective counterbalance. By his centring his approach on this incarnational basis he brought this whole teaching back into proportion, involving the whole human being and not just the 'mind'.

Here, quite plainly, the term *hesychia*, or silence, quietness, has come to mean the solitary, contemplative life of a monk practising a specific way of prayer. This prayer is marked by a compunction and penitence. It has the sense of a kind of joyful mourning of one's own and the world's pitiableness. It knows our need to be rescued and saved, with tears. It is expressed in short, urgently or longingly repeated prayer directed to Jesus present in the heart, a presence to which the person praying seeks to turn his or her waking and sleeping thoughts ('I slept but my heart was awake', Song of Solomon 5:2), and whole life. The prayer might be the *kyrie*, 'Lord have mercy' or Cassian's 'O God make speed to save us, haste O God to help us' or any variant, (a wide range of biblical verses are used) or a cry for help. But it is always, above all, a 'remembrance' of Jesus.

There is even here a hint of later breathing exer-

43

cises. 'When you unite the memory of Jesus with your breathing, then you will know the benefit of *hesychia*.' John Climacus echoes Diadochus and other earlier writers. 'With every breath remember Jesus.' 'Renew the memory of Jesus.' 'Smite your enemies with the name of Jesus...'. He even mentions 'recalling, as you go to sleep and as you wake up, the memory of death' and with it the one word (*monologistos*) prayer of Jesus. This is perhaps the first actual reference to the 'Jesus Prayer'. But this would still seem to mean *any* short repeated prayer that is directed to Jesus, provided that it is always a prayer of compunction, with something about it of a plea for forgiveness and mercy.

Though this means a struggle to attain to uninterrupted worship and petition, set in a life of austere discipline, fasting and the like, of physical work and of corporate, mutual caring, the 'hesychast' enters more and more into a communion of the whole person with the transfigured Christ and aspires 'to approach the incorporeal from within a fleshly dwelling...'.

Such is the experience which informs the theology of Maximus the Confessor (580–662) as he shows the goal of life to be love, and the path to that goal to be communion with God which in turn will bring with it liberation from the passions, the reuniting of the divided nature of human beings and the transforming of *eros* (desiring love) into *agape* (self-giving love).

Increasingly, where the practice of this 'hesychastic' prayer prevailed at all, the name of Jesus came to be specifically used and the prayer itself began to take a more fixed form. St Hesychios of Batos, a monk of Mount Sinai in the seventh century, who

45

drew upon St John of the Ladder, loved to borrow his phrases and to embellish his teaching poetically, 'As water ripples with a light breeze, so does the Holy Spirit move in the depths of the heart, making us cry out "Abba, Father!"' He refers to the 'prayer *of* Jesus' (*Jesu euche*) and speaks of *'clinging* with your memory to the name of Jesus'.

'Attention and incessant *hesychia* of the heart... continual uninterrupted breathing and calling upon Christ Jesus, Son of God and God Himself.' He speaks of the Jesus prayer clinging to the breath and of the soul clinging to the Jesus Prayer, breathing in the power and wisdom of God the Father who is Jesus Christ.

'To the breath of your nostrils unite attention (*nepsis*) and the name of Jesus, as well as meditation on death and complete humility...'. 'Truly happy is the man in whom the Jesus Prayer clings to the power of thought and who calls on him continually in his heart, in the way that our body is united to the atmosphere or a flame to the candle wick.'

It is clear that this was still, for several centuries, to be only one kind of prayer among others, still unknown in many parts of the Eastern Church and not even being used on Mount Athos until the early fourteenth century. But its distinctive pattern and focus had been established. Henceforth, from Maximus on, the outlines were drawn of a vision of God and of the world which sprang out of an incarnational root, and was nourished by the experience of contemplative prayer.

8

The Jesus Prayer from the fourteenth to the twentieth centuries

The scene shifts finally from the desert tradition and the monasteries and hermits of Sinai to Byzantium where much doctrine in the more worldly and secularized atmosphere of the imperial city had become over-rationalized under the influence of philosophy and where there was need of a fresh realization of the vision of God.

Symeon the New Theologian (949–1022) was the prophet of such a movement with the same stress upon the encounter with the incarnate Christ as the hesychasts. Although he did not refer to the Jesus Prayer nor describe a similar method, he sought to ground theology in the experience of personal communion with God as the hesychasts had done. His teaching and his writing were centred upon his experience of Christ and of the reality of his kingdom in prayer. Now the kingdom begins.

For Symeon, the resurrection is not only in the future. It begins here and now. His poems and meditations were to seize the imagination of generations of Eastern Christians and to shape their tradition. He wrote out of an overwhelming encounter with the living Christ and with the Holy Spirit, through whom he claimed the resurrection of all of us can occur. Exiled from Byzantium, only to be restored and vindicated at the end of his life, we must not forget that he was, despite being so controversial, a lasting influence on Eastern thought and that he was the supreme example, as the title he was given deliberately suggests, of the claim, in that tradition, that the true theologian is he who prays. This was to become an important theme in later history, a theme with which the Jesus Prayer itself was to become interwoven.

'Being in a state of illumination, the holy man is completely on fire with the Holy Spirit, and… in this anticipates the mystery of his deification,' wrote his biographer, Nicetas Stethatos. He is speaking here of the hope of all the hesychasts which Symeon himself made so real again, that we shall through prayer and sacrament and growth in love be finally 'in Christ', be made 'partakers of the Divine nature, brought body and soul into intimate communion with the Threefold God'. It is striking that that same biographer himself recommended 'the invocation of the Jesus-God', urging his readers to put to flight the assaults of evil fantasies by 'making the life-giving sign of the cross and calling on Jesus-God'.

After this there is one of those 'tunnel periods' in the history of the Jesus Prayer, in which all we are given is occasional glimpses and references here and there of various forms of the prayer. Even within the lifetime of Symeon, hesychastic prayer seems to have gone underground and its meaning and particular forms quite widely lost to view. There were one or two references at the Byzantine court: a prince who had become a monk, Abba Isaiah, the spiritual director of the twelfth-century Emperor's daughter; St Meletius, a wandering hesychast. St Meletius is described as saying the prayer, 'Lord Jesus Christ, Son of God, have mercy upon me'. But very little else is known about the prayer at this time.

Then, in the late thirteenth and the fourteenth centuries, a new flowering of the tradition suddenly began on Mount Athos itself. A patriarch and the Metropolitan of Philadelphia were among those beginning to develop and codify the prayer elsewhere. Before them Nikephoras, an Italian who became a monk on Mount Athos, gave the movement a fresh impetus there.

But it was St Gregory of Sinai (Gregory 'the Sinaite', died 1346) who became a more well-known influence on Mount Athos. Having received instruction on how to pray the Jesus Prayer from a monk in Crete, he went on to raise up a new generation of those who would pray in this way on the holy mountain. He prescribed a method of praying the prayer and at least two ways of saying it ('Lord Jesus Christ, have mercy on me', followed by 'Son of God, have mercy on me'). He became a far-reaching influence. Even St Nilus of Sora ('Nil Sorski') the first great hesychast in Russia (1433–1508), who visited the East for thirteen years from 1465, imbibed much of St Gregory's teaching during his time on Mount Athos and took it back to Russia where generations of monks were brought up on his writing. St Gregory's friend at Athos, St Maximus of Kapsokalyvia received the gift of unceasing prayer as he was standing praying at the ikon of the Virgin, and seems symbolic of the new fervour for the Jesus Prayer which began to spread through the Eastern Empire. At the end of the fourteenth century two writers,

Kallistos, Patriarch of Constantinople in 1397, and Ignatios Xanthopoulos produced an anthology of the writings of their predecessors which was called *The Century*. A fragment from a little later was also attributed to Kallistos which describes the use of the words 'My Jesus!' as an exclamation of prayer used 'when the mind becomes intensely attached to the Divine influence'. With their work the Byzantine cycle ended.

For the most part, this revival of the prayer at the end of the Byzantine period was more strictly identified with one form of words—'Lord Jesus Christ, Son of God, have mercy upon me'. Near the end of the period, the words 'a sinner' were sometimes added at the end. This prayer was now usually accompanied by a particular bodily posture, as prescribed by St Gregory the Sinaite, the head lowered and the eyes gazing down at the heart, together with a particular way of breathing (often this entitled breathing 'in' on the first half of the prayer, and 'out' on the second) which had not been prescribed in earlier times. Once again it was seen, along with baptism and communion, as a way into union with God in Christ in the Spirit even in this life. Grace and peace and even palpable light would infuse the body and soul of those who wholeheartedly espoused this prayer. There was above all a strong emphasis on the original biblical and incarnational basis of the Christian life. The emphasis on posture or on breathing were supremely meant to help the person praying to 'keep one's mind in one's heart' and to yield one's whole bodily being to be drawn into the life of the threefold God. The only entry into this re-union must be, as in the desert tradition, through a continuous penitence or mourning.

Over against such a theology rooted in prayer and the gradually transfigured life described by St Symeon, there was in Byzantium at that time another very different teaching. This was the then fashionable philosophical, humanist tradition represented by, amongst others, a certain Barlaam of Calabria. Influenced partly by a sophisticated Western philosophy (Italian humanism derived from Aristotle and some Neoplatonism), Barlaam was trying to give Christian thought an acceptable rational basis. He looked not so much to direct experience of God as to an approach through the creation, more of a natural theology, since God was inaccessible to the human mind.

The monks and their practices and their teaching shocked him as barbaric and almost superstitious. The notion of a theology arising from a way of prayer was difficult for him to comprehend. He denounced hesychasm as crude and literal, and the monks as 'navel gazers'!

Through St Gregory Palamas (1296–1359) the Jesus Prayer once again—as in the early days of the desert and the crucial contribution of Bishop Diadochus of Photike—became the symbol of a biblical, incarnational approach to truth. He became the philosopher and thus the theologian of the whole hesychast tradition as we have seen it develop. When he was visiting Thessalonica, Palamas was approached by some local monks to help defend their spirituality and faith against the attacks of Barlaam which were beginning to gain influential support in the capital. Inspired by his own experience of prayer gained on Mount Athos when he was a young man, a ten-year period of solitary prayer and a time as an abbot, Palamas took up his pen and wrote the famous *Triads*. These were a defence of the vital claim that God is only disclosed through profound personal experience of a transfiguration. He agreed with Barlaam that God cannot be known by reason. He agreed that we can only approach God through a *via negativa*, a negative way, in which all our first assumptions are stripped from us as we advance like Moses on the mountain into the darkness of the cloud surrounding God. But that very experience of being stripped of all that we thought we were, of losing life to save it, is in truth a process of repentance, a change of mind as well as heart, a crucial *metanoia*, which brings us step by step not into an empty darkness but into the very presence of the living God.

We are thus capable of being transfigured by the Spirit of God through communion with Christ. By faith and in the darkness of the repentance of our own heart and mind we can transcend our own nature. We are, as Meyendorff puts it, admitted to true vision when we cease to see. This is nothing less than a philosophy of the Jesus Prayer!

It was crucial that this teaching became a part of the accepted tradition of Orthodoxy in the East and in Russia. It was brought to Russia by the man who came to be known as St Nilus of Sora, or 'Nil Sorsky,' whom I have already mentioned. He was the first great Russian man of prayer. As a young monk he had entered one of the early larger monasteries in Russia, set on a mountain in the northern forests near the famous 'White Lake' in about 1425. In 1465 he managed to carry out a long-cherished plan of visiting the Orthodox East, Constantinople—which had fallen into Muslim hands twelve years earlier—the Holy Land and Mount Athos. He absorbed the teaching of the two Gregories, Palamas and 'the Sinaite', who taught on Mount Athos that the Jesus Prayer, prayed 'with the mind in the heart' ignoring all other (even good) thoughts gradually gave control of the passions and became the channel of the healing fire of the Holy Spirit—grace itself, warming and illuminating the soul, stopping sinful thoughts and filling our fleshly being with light. Nilus, inspired by this teaching, returned to Russia in 1478.

Just as Russia was consciously developing into the 'new Byzantium', the would-be heir to the old, vanished Empire of the East, Nilus transmitted something of the very essence of the hesychastic tradition of the Eastern monks and spiritual Fathers (and Mothers). In the depths of the primal forests of the north, he established his 'skete', a community of small hermits' huts, with a common chapel and meeting place. It was modelled, like so many of the Celtic settlements in Ireland and Britain, on the communal life of the old Egyptian hermit monks in the desert of Scetis, hence the name. Here the pinewood forests of the north became the new desert, and the hermits on the banks of the river Sora the heirs to the long-lived 'counterculture' of the Eastern monks and solitaries.

In Nilus' great work, *The Tradition of the Scetic Life*, he stored up all the treasures of his new 'Athos', where everyone prayed and worked in their own cell, told of the way to overcome the passions and to grow into union with God through repentant prayer. He included an anthology of the spiritual writings of the Eastern teachers of prayer in which he was so well versed, and recommended the Jesus Prayer as Gregory the Sinaite had described it, keeping 'the mind in the heart' and breathing slowly, until some attain to that state which lies beyond prayer and seems almost one with the life of the kingdom of God. Although this work was so widely copied in many monasteries, and both monks and nuns became fervent disciples of St Nilus—often as much opposed to the worldliness of monasteries as much as of the rest of the Church—they tended to be scattered and hidden and the whole tradition went somewhat underground. Nilus' writings were still known by some and there were those amongst the impressive line of people of prayer and sanctity keeping the flame burning through the sixteenth and seventeenth centuries, who knew the Jesus Prayer. But it was not until the eighteenth century that the great tradition began to be revived.

Once again, at a moment when all spirituality was under attack, both the Church and monasticism were at a low ebb and both under increasing attack from the government itself, the Jesus Prayer began to emerge from the tunnel. The increasing scepticism of the age of the so-called 'Enlightenment' and ultimately the division between rationalism and romanticism, heart and head, seemed to require a rediscovery of that true integrity of spirit of which the incarnation is the real pledge. The Jesus Prayer, and the whole spiritual inheritance of which it had become the heart and symbol, were the key to that rediscovery of 'God in Christ' and of the Holy Spirit.

Mount Athos itself, like other parts of Christendom, had suffered from apathy and decay during this period but it soon became the setting for an intense reactivation of the Jesus Prayer. A refugee bishop, St Macarius of Corinth, driven out from his bishopric by the Turkish authorities, after a wandering life arrived at Mount Athos, encountered there one of the most profoundly learned and spiritual writers of the century, Nicodemus of Naxos (the 'Hagiorite') who had been praying and studying on the holy mountain. They were both interested in Western theological works and translated them together. Macarius left and then returned in 1784. It was then that they completed another project begun earlier, that of compiling a complete anthology of writings on the Jesus Prayer. This became the famous *Philokalia* or 'Love of Beauty' (meaning 'spiritual beauty'), the quest for unification with God through faith and unceasing prayer. The great book was published in Greek in Venice and soon began to spread its influence.

Earlier in the century, Paisius Velichovsky, after wanderings which led him away from Russia and into the Polish Ukraine and Romanian Moldavia, came to live and work under a remarkable *staretz*, or elder, called Onuphrius, in a remote and austere skete in the mountains like that of Nilus of Sora. Gradually he realized that all the works they were studying on prayer came from Mount Athos. So he resolved to go there. In the end he found himself in the 1750s on the mountain, at the head of a movement, as the *staretz* and 'willy-nilly abbot' to a growing community of Russian monks and seekers. Remarkably he managed to take them back with him to Moldavia, seek for larger and better accommodation, and eventually, with his monks, to settle in Neamtu. Here he did much to translate Greek Orthodox literature on prayer. Eventually in 1791 he produced his translation of the *Philokalia* which he called *Dobrotolubyie*, 'Love of Good'. This book and its new editions in 1822 and 1842 became the great classical *Summa* for monks in Russia of all teaching about the Jesus Prayer. This prayer, for Paisius, was union between God and humanity. A great mass of Russian pilgrims had fled from the oppressive atmosphere of eighteenth-century Russia to Romania, and we are told that by 1778 Paisius had a thousand monks in his monastery. Most of these returned to Russia in the last years of the century and began a revival of not only Russian monasticism but of hesychasm, the use and teaching of the Jesus Prayer, and what became a golden age of Russian spirituality.

All the great spiritual figures of the nineteenth century in Russia—like their descendants in the persecutions and prison camps of the twentieth, or in exile on Mount Athos, men such as St Silouan, the inspirer of Sophrony, the founder of the monastery I went to—looked to the *Philokalia* or the *Dobrotolubyie* and tended to practise the Jesus Prayer.

St Seraphim of Sarov, in the early nineteenth century, after years of solitude in a little hut, with his bees, deep in the forest, 'praying on a stone, for a thousand nights and days', kneeling and reciting 'the prayer of the Publican, "God have mercy on me, a sinner"', and after being attacked by robbers, returned to seclusion in his monastery. Then after five years he came out to meet with people and counsel them, and at length went back to pray the prayer in a hermitage in the forest nearer at hand.

Bishop Ignatius Bryanchaninov was an outstanding commentator on the Jesus Prayer. After loyal service to the Tsar as both an army officer from a wealthy family and later an abbot of Sergiev monastery close to the imperial palace, he was appointed Bishop of the Caucasus and the Black Sea (1858–1898). He soon retreated from his diocese to become a recluse and wrote at length on the Jesus Prayer. Similarly Bishop Theophan the Recluse, teacher and then rector of St Petersburg Academy before becoming Bishop of Tambov, then Vladimir, retired to a monastery to pray and to write. He did this for twenty-eight years and during this time he developed some of the most profound and striking contemplative theology in the whole history of the Jesus Prayer.

It is equally striking that the three great spiritual fathers of the monastery of Optino—made famous as it was by their outstanding distinction as spiritual counsellors to so many Russians in the later nineteenth century, including Tolstoy, Soloviev and Dostoyevsky among other intellectuals—should have been rooted in a community which drew great strength from the *Dobrotolubyie*. The great anthology was in the Optino library from the beginning of the century and the monastery continued in its tradition to beyond that century's end.

This presence of the Jesus Prayer in the very heart of the life of Optino points to its power once again to encapsulate a crucial resistance of the personal communion with God in Christ to all the underlying disintegration which in the nineteenth century threatened to distract and disintegrate human life. In 1831 St Seraphim of Sarov, shining out in the dark forests of his retreat, as the snow fell softly far around, had prophesied to his disciple Motovilov—a man whom he had healed. Motovilov, in a famous conversation, recorded for posterity the words in which the radiant *staretz* (elder or spiritual guide) foretold something of the travail of the century to come and promised the power and protection of the Holy Spirit.

LORD JESUS CHRIST
SON OF GOD

Lord Jesus

Christ Son of God
have mercy
on me

Lord Jesus Christ Son of God have mercy on us

Lord Jesus Christ Son of God have mercy on us

HAVE MERCY
ON ME

But now through the deepening underlying upheaval of the years leading up to the First World War and the Russian Revolution, in a time of social and spiritual and intellectual ferment, Optino in turn was to shine out into the troubled hearts and minds of many. Dostoyevsky expounded his analysis of the essential contradictions, illusions and tragic self-deception of modern (and so called 'postmodern') society. No wonder his earlier writings and his bitterly sceptical presentation of modern society so much appealed to Nietzsche. But in *The Brothers Karamazov* alongside this dark view of the human tragedy he presented an alternative vision of another possibility. Over against the ultimate nihilism so overwhelmingly embodied in Ivan Karamazov he set the frail integrity of his younger brother Alyosha, disciple of Father Zossima, himself a portrayal of Amvrosy or Ambrose, the greatest of the Optino *startzy*. Alyosha sets out from the monastery to bear his indestructible message of the marriage of heaven and earth in Jesus, pledge of the reality of the divine mercy, into a precarious world. Continuous repentance and even more continuous forgiveness are all that he has to bring. And at the heart of the way of prayer and love which is his only protection flows the Jesus Prayer. He is a kind of prototype of those who will live this prayer through all the great catastrophes, the deserts of pain and slaughter and all the concentration camps and gulags that stretch ahead.

In post-revolutionary Russia itself, others in each generation were to make the discovery offered in Alyosha. Father Sophrony himself was one of these as he found his way through a kind of new-age-style Eastern philosophizing and mysticism from

Moscow to Paris to Mount Athos and so to the great intercessor for humanity in these tragic times, St Silouan who there, in the 1920s and early 1930s, taught him the Jesus Prayer. And through him, as through so many other exiles, and through translations (like that of the diary of a nineteenth-century Russian seeker, *The Way of a Pilgrim*, published in 1930), the tradition, the literature and the form of the Jesus Prayer began to penetrate the West.

9

What happens when you pray the Jesus Prayer

From this outline of the history you realize that there have been many different versions of the prayer from its beginnings, and that in the early days there were many different verses of the Bible and phrases that people used to use in the same kind of way, addressing the prayer 'with the mind in the heart' to Jesus. Such prayers were always a kind of 'practice of the presence of Jesus'. The essence of the prayer was to seek to come into his presence and to stay there until eventually you were always conscious of that presence and always in communion with him. That was the goal. In seeking this presence you would have to recognize all the passions that struggle to take hold of you in the depths of your being constantly. You have to keep turning from them to Christ and keep letting his presence with you and in you through the Holy Spirit still these passions and transform them into energies working for good.

In *The Great Divorce*, C.S. Lewis has a magnificent passage about a man whose lust is like a hideous lizard clinging to his shoulder and holding him back. But as he lets himself be taken upwards it is transformed into a beautiful horse onto which he leaps up and so rides into heaven. This is exactly the way in which our growth into the presence and love of God in Christ through the Spirit will gradually enable the dark, shadow side of ourselves to be drawn into light.

The classical form which the Jesus Prayer finally took in the fourteenth century was 'Lord Jesus Christ, Son of God, have mercy on me, a sinner.' The last words, 'a sinner', were only added by some and only, of course, when the prayer was being said by one person on his or her own, which has been the normal practice. Even then some people include the phrase 'Son of God' and some, like the Russian pilgrim in the little green book I mentioned, leave it out. Some add the adjective 'living' to God: 'Son of the *living* God'. All these variations are of little importance. But it does seem that the classical form, as it was taught to me by people like Archimandirite Sophrony at the monastery, has a kind of completeness. It keeps the prayer entirely trinitarian, and it preserves its double nature as prayer of adoration and praise and joy in the entering over and over again into the presence and recollection of God— 'Lord Jesus Christ, Son of God'—and also prayer of total confession and surrender and yearning for wholeness—'have mercy on me, a sinner'. Each half of the prayer then has a balancing number of beats, if you include 'of' with the word 'God' and 'a' with 'sinner'. But these are small and debatable points. The most important thing, I am sure, is, as one of the early teachers wrote, to decide the form of the prayer which you are going to use and then stick to it. It will not grow if it is constantly being uprooted and changed.

In the fourteenth century a new emphasis was laid also on making the prayer part of your breathing, taking literally what much earlier teachers like John Climacus had only meant far more broadly and symbolically when they talked of uniting the prayer with each breath. And of course it is possible to breathe in as you say the words of the first half of the prayer and out as you say the words of the second. The first half then becomes an inviting in of God, as it were, and the second both a sigh of sorrow and of longing to be enfolded in the mercy and lovingkindness of God in Christ, and an expelling of the old to bring in the new. But it is significant that the main teachers of the prayer in more recent times, people like Theophan the Recluse, urge us to forget about breathing in special ways, apart from breathing slowly as a general aspect of relaxing and becoming still.

Again some have suggested coordinating the pace and rhythm of praying the prayer with the pace and rhythm of your heart, so that each beat of the prayer goes with a beat of the pulse or the heart. But again I think many wise teachers would suggest that even that can be too contrived and can make you too self-conscious. Perhaps it is better to pray the prayer spontaneously and to just let it well up as it will. In all these minor details—as in the form of the prayer you decide to use—it is best to take up whatever you find useful and not to worry about the rest. Above all it is best to stay with what you have settled upon and get on with it.

I have found it useful to use the knotted prayer cord which Orthodox monks use and which I was given. They call it in Russian a 'tchotki' or in Greek, *komvoschoinion*. It often has a hundred knots in it. You say the prayer once with each knot. At intervals in the cord, often at the twenty-fifth point, there is a wooden bead. When you reach that bead you can pause and be silent, or sometimes intercede specifically for those laid on your heart and perhaps written in your prayer notebook. I keep a tiny looseleaf book for that purpose. One can of course put the name of such a person in place of 'me' as you repeat the prayer.

Bishop Kallistos has written what is to me far and away the best book on the Jesus Prayer for practical purposes, *The Power of the Name*. In it he, too, suggests (page 28) interceding by putting the name of the person or people you are praying for in place of 'me, a sinner' at the end of the prayer, just as in the monastery they often shift to 'have mercy upon us and upon our world'. However, for my own part I find it easier to remember the people separately, thinking of them, within the framework of the prayer, but to stick to the same phrases all the time. After all, the whole prayer becomes an intercession. Soon I find that I am no longer praying just for myself, but when I say 'on me, a sinner' I find that all the situations of grief and terror, of pain and suffering begin to be drawn into me and I into them. I begin to pray as a fragment of this wounded creation longing for its release into fulfilment. The *macro*cosm of the world and the *micro*cosm of my own heart look curiously similar and become part of each other. I am in those for whom I would pray and they are in me, as is the whole universe. Every petition of the prayer becomes a bringing of all into the presence and love of God. But I am leaping ahead and will return to this at the finish.

There is just one more point to make before we come to the praying of the prayer. I felt that I needed, in embarking on this new way of praying, the help of someone to whom I could talk from time to time about how it was going; someone who would be able to guide me and encourage me. I think that when we seek to go more deeply into prayer it is best to have a 'soul friend' as the Celtic tradition called such a person, someone with whom you can take counsel. Many teachers of the prayer have urged that one should have a *staretz*, an elder, to help one. And if they could not find one they sought for help in reading earlier writers in an anthology such as the *Philokalia*. It is good to read more about this way of praying as well. I list some books I have found helpful at the end of this book. I also found out just how important it was that I had a regular place in a worshipping community, and indeed in a home group. This was part of the vital framework that became more necessary than ever.

I also found that it was good to have the daily time of morning and evening prayer and Bible reading as part of that framework. Even a short daily prayer with a reading from the Bible becomes a vital part of the whole growth into a deeper union with God and a fuller active discipleship day by day which we are seeking through the Jesus Prayer.

After such a time of reading and praying, using some kind of order of prayer, however simple and brief, and of dwelling on a Bible passage, preferably using some commentary or indeed Bible reading notes such as *New Daylight*, or in the evening perhaps, reading a book about prayer for a short time, I would put all books aside.

Sometimes when you want to pray you don't quite know where to begin. You go into a quiet place, or into a church which happens to be open. And you kneel down, and you aren't sure what to do next.

There's the silence and there's you. And one of the great strengths of the Jesus Prayer is that it gives you something… a stream that you can very gently enter into. You start saying the prayer, and you can be quite leisurely about it. You don't want to be rushed. What you want is to be relaxed. And, as in all prayer, whether you are sitting or kneeling, to be both still and alert, both relaxed and alert. Still but also at rest so that you are watchful, but you are also restful.

The Jesus Prayer has always been seen and experienced as a stilling, and it is good to be still as you pray. That doesn't mean that you can't scratch your ear, or move if you are uncomfortable. It is just a matter of trying to calm down and to be quiet and to breathe gently.

I have found it best to kneel and then put one of those low prayer stools just behind you and sit back on it. Some prefer to sit upright on a chair, their legs uncrossed, their feet not far apart, their hands resting on their knees. I then try to keep as upright and straight-backed as I can, with that blend of restfulness and alertness of body which helps you to concentrate on the prayer. Seek to find a comfortable position and then be absolutely still, breathing gently and relaxing every part of your body.

I begin by saying as meaningfully as I can in my mind 'In the name of the Father and of the Son and of the Holy Spirit', calling upon and placing myself as it were in the loving hold upon me of the Triune God. And I ask the Holy Spirit to pray within me and to unite me through the Son with the Father.

Then I launch out into the prayer, letting the flow of the Spirit bear me and seeking to turn in heart and mind to God. The constant emphasis has been from the beginning on praying 'with the mind in the heart'. The 'heart' here is seen as the true centre of my own being, the place from which my deepest feelings arise, the place from which I am truly motivated in whatever I seek to do, the place where spontaneously I know what is really moving me at this moment. The 'mind' is the mental activity of both framing the words of the prayer and turning to the thought of the presence of God in the person of Jesus Christ within me and around me through the Spirit. As I say the words of the prayer I seek to recall that presence, to recognize that love reaching out to me, and then to 'want to want' to respond with my whole being. I try to look to him inwardly as— through invoking his name and realizing that he is within me and his name named upon me through my very baptism—I recognize slowly, dimly, that he is here, closer to me than I am to myself. Even if I can feel little, I repeat the prayer steadily with a brief pause between each articulation of it, neither hurriedly nor too slowly. The heartbeat when we are quite still can in fact indicate the right pace.

The early practitioners and teachers of the prayer all stressed the importance of speaking out loud to start with, so that the person praying was formulating the words and getting completely used to them. So did the Russian teachers in the nineteenth century. And to do that was to use the top of the mind and give it an activity to occupy itself with as the fingers are given an activity by the use of the prayer cord. Meanwhile the heart must seek actively to draw near to God and to open itself to the Spirit. That is what happens in all spoken, repeated prayer, even in morning and evening prayer in the Offices. What matters is this sense of getting into a repeated prayer and underlying it into the closer union of thought and feeling with God. Of course this idea of saying the prayer aloud was formed in an era when people read aloud even when they were reading to themselves, and were far less used to silent reading on their own than we are today. We would now move very much more quickly into saying the prayer silently in our own minds. But sometimes speaking the prayer to start with does prove helpful in getting into the flow of it and establishing its movement in your own consciousness.

The hesychastic teachers all insisted on the continuous effort that has to be made when we are first embarking on the prayer. They said that the work of inner prayer consisted in making oneself pray the prayer continually with one's mouth, without ceasing, 'Lord Jesus Christ, Son of God, have mercy upon me, [a sinner].'

My mind very soon wanders all over the place. I find I have been reciting the prayer mechanically with my thoughts elsewhere. But I *know* now that this is entirely natural. The invocation of the name 'Lord Jesus Christ' very soon becomes a way of being constantly recalled to that loving presence. After every wander I keep returning, turning to him. I realize more and more that our whole life is a constant turning again—*metanoia*, which we have translated 'repentance'. So it seems natural and right to continue 'have mercy on me'. And yet it is never a kind of continual grovelling in our sins, a kind of self-flagellation, as it might appear to be at first. It is essentially a cry for help and a cry of longing to be grasped in his great love.

To recollect his presence is, from the first, light and peace. He comes not in reproach, not in rebuke for our constant absence and betrayal, but in joy that we are with him! I often think of the moment when he appeared in the Upper Room to the astonished disciples, huddled together in despair, the doors locked for fear, nothing in the past but the knowledge of their own failure, nothing in the future but the loss of him, like waking from a dream into a deserted world. Suddenly he is with them. And his first words are not, 'Where were you when I needed you? You have let me down!' His first words are, 'Shalom [that peace which enfolds heaven and earth and brings everything and everyone back into their right place] be with you.' He shows them his hands and his side. They can recognize that it is he and that the wounds are healed, and he has passed through death itself. His love is final after all. 'Then the disciples rejoiced when they saw the Lord' (John 20:19–20).

This is the fundamental reality of the prayer and of our faith. We start by coming home to him. In his presence we may be glad, we may give thanks, we may be filled with happiness and with enjoyment of everything. The first movement in prayer is always that of being received into the welcoming embrace of one who is waiting to receive us gladly and of realizing afresh that we are loved and cherished. We have to learn to dwell within this reality. As Watchman Nee wrote long ago in one of his marvellous books of 'primitive' theology (analogous to primitive painting), his study of Ephesians: 'Sit—Walk—Stand'. We have to start by sitting, by being 'raised up to dwell with him in heavenly places'. Later we shall begin to walk 'in him' and so come to be able to 'stand'. In our prayer we always go back to the beginning and let him reach out to lift us up, like the servant fallen into a ditch in Julian of

Norwich's picture of humankind. I used sometimes to say, 'Lord Jesus Christ, Love of God...' to remind me of this.

So our prayer begins over and over again in the joy of the one who welcomes us, lifts us up, and breathes his Spirit into us, as at the beginning in the first creation, that Spirit by which 'the love of God is shed abroad in our hearts'. It is a prayer of thanksgiving for the whole creation and for being brought into life to be a part of it. We are drawn into the presence of Christ and into the life of God.

As we go on to 'have mercy on me, a sinner' we are filled with sorrow both for our own sin and failure and for the sin and suffering of the world. The mood is one of what John Climacus called 'joyful mourning' or, in Bishop Kallistos' words, 'joy-creating sorrow'. There is a repentance here, just as the disciples in the Upper Room may have seen the radiance of the one who greeted them with such complete happiness refracted through their tears. But there is also a sense of entering into a movement of redemption constantly at work not only in the microcosm of our own hearts but also in the macrocosm of the universe.

I have found an amazing sense, as I prayed this prayer continuously, of being drawn into this movement of grace perpetually at work in everyone and in all things. Even in the natural universe, there would seem to be a constant emergence of a new organization and order out of seemingly total disorder. I always think of the way in which after the bombing of Coventry, someone wandering in the smoking ruins of the beautiful old late medieval cathedral, its matchless clerestories and slender pillars now reduced to heaps of rubble, suddenly saw in a grouping of the medieval nails scattered on the ground the tiny form of a cross and saw in it the clue to a new meaning, the possibility of creating a new structure, building a new, 'kindlier, more Christ-like world' out of the wreckage of the old. The cross became the sign of a universal turning.

This is the theme of the work of the great Nobel prizewinner, Ilya Prigogine, who has studied, in many physical, chemical and biological processes, the strange emergence of new organization and complexity out of seeming total disorder. From the first beginnings of the creation of our universe, out of disintegration, again and again a fresh impulse from without sets off a tremendous upheaval, out of which, often with surprising suddenness, a new and marvellous patterning comes into being. A complex new order arises. From the famous 'big bang' on, there was possibly a great break in the symmetry and equilibrium which up to that moment had prevailed, a disintegration into myriads of particles. Then out of a series of similar breakdowns, each irreversible, energy was again and again released, and out of this release suddenly there arose fresh organization, a series of new patternings.

Could this picture give us fresh insight into the way in which Jesus is indeed, as in Ephesians and Colossians, the cosmic Christ, his dying and being raised up being the enactment of the way in which the whole divine purpose is always being realized in and through everything? Certainly with the seemingly miraculous emergence of human consciousness in the further development of this constant order out of chaos, we see the possibility of a new form, a new level of moral and spiritual life coming into being. And through the inchoate efforts of

71

human societies to arrive at some universal forms of order and freedom there seems yet again the sense that only through a constant rhythm of repentance and forgiveness, reorientation and reconstruction, can we keep struggling our way towards our ever elusive goal.

As I have prayed the Jesus Prayer continuously, morning and evening, and it has begun to start 'praying itself', as it were; at other times both in the night and in the day, at odd moments, walking or cycling, in the car, or even in the stillness between two conversations, it has assumed more and more the form of some kind of a universal rhythm. The stream of the loving purpose encapsulated in the prayer seems gradually to be uniting the prayer with all the tragic struggles of our world and of wounded nature itself. It seems to make the person praying a part of that movement of new creation.

Intercession then comes naturally into the constant tidal action of the prayer. You find yourself alternating at the points of pause for intercession between the ongoing flow of the prayer and the particular person or situation which the prayer at that time is embracing for you and through you. There seems to be a perfectly fitting alternation between the two moments of the ongoing universal stream of prayer and the special concrete need of a particular person or situation.

I frequently find myself caught up into a particular situation which has presented itself to me through one of my visits or journeys, through a television programme, the news perhaps, through a newspaper or a letter from someone. I turn to it and then find I have to go back into the prayer and then later the situation presents itself again. There is an interesting Russian precedent for that kind of alternation, and it is in the story of St Silouan as it has been told by Father Sophrony and quoted by Archbishop Anthony Bloom in one of his books on prayer. It describes how Silouan was in charge of one of the workshops of the Russian monastery on Mount Athos.

He was the steward of the monastery at the time and he had to look after its domestic affairs. There was a workshop on the estate, and the people who worked in it were all Russian peasants, as Silouan himself had been. They were lay people who had come to do a job in this place because there was no work in Russia. They would send the money they earned back to their families, whom they had had to leave behind.

Every day Silouan went to this workshop and gave the workers the tasks that they were going to do. And he would take a great interest in them. After he had got them organized he would go back to his cell and then start praying the Jesus Prayer. Then he thinks about a particular man, and his wife and children back in Russia, and the difficulty of having to come all this way and being separated from them—and wondering how they are going to manage without him.

> When he came in in the morning he would
> never enter the workshop without having
> prayed for the people there. He would come
> with his heart filled with compassion and
> love for them. He would have tears in his
> soul for love of them. He would give them
> the task they had to perform and then while
> they were working he would go into his cell

and pray for each of them individually. He described himself praying for one:

'He is young. He is just 20. He has left in his village his wife who is even younger than he is and their first child. Can you imagine the misery of those there, that he has had to leave them because they could not survive on his work at home.

'Protect them in his absence! Shield them against every evil! Give him courage to struggle through this year and go back to the joy of a meeting with enough money but also the courage the face the difficulties.' And he said:

'In the beginning I prayed with tears of compassion for Nicholas, for his young wife and little child. But as I was praying the sense of the divine presence began to grow on me, and at a certain moment it grew so powerful that I lost sight of Nicholas, his wife, his child, his needs and their village and I could be aware only of God.

'And I was drawn by the sense of the divine presence deeper and deeper until all of a sudden at the heart of this presence [when, he says, 'drawn by a sense of the divine presence', he is praying the Jesus Prayer] I met the divine love holding Nicholas, his wife and his child. And it was with the love of God that I began to pray.

'And again I was drawn into the deep, and in the depths I again found the divine love. And so I spend my days praying for each of them in turn. One after the other. And when the day is over I say a few words

to them, and we pray together and they go to
their rest. And I go back to fulfil my
monastic office.'

I immediately recognized the truth of that story in
my own much lesser experience. Through the alternation of universal and particular into which both
the rejoicing and the yearning of the Jesus Prayer
had brought me, I found it possible to intercede at
more depth than I had known before for many people and situations. People who would themselves
have felt very far from God and who were often bitterly alienated from all that they associated with the
very notion, and even people who would bitterly
repudiate any such prayer for them could be encom-
passed in this intercession. It was almost as if the
flow of the prayer itself touched upon and drew in
more than I knew or would ever know of the suffering and frustration of the whole groaning creation.

St Silouan himself became one of the very great
intercessors of our time, I am quite certain. 'Upon
your walls, O Jerusalem, I have posted sentinels; all
day and all night they shall never be silent. You who
remind the Lord, take no rest, and give him no rest
until he establishes Jerusalem and makes it
renowned throughout the earth' (Isaiah 62:6–7).

For Silouan sin and the demonic darkness that lies
over us like a thick veil had oppressed him sorely in
his early years in the monastery. At one time he was
so savagely assaulted by demonic powers, as it
seemed, surrounding him, that he felt like St Antony
or one of the other early Desert Fathers, almost over-
whelmed. In answer to the question how these
assailants could be taken from him, he felt God reply
to him in his heart, 'The proud always suffer.' Then

when he asked how this pride could be taken from him he received the enigmatic and haunting reply, 'Keep thy mind in Hell and despair not.' It was after that, that pressing on in prayer through the continuing tunnel of this darkness, he began to recognize that it was in part the oppression of the absence of the sense of God and the alienation from his love over the whole face of the globe. He had been called himself to undergo this travail not just on account of his own sin alone any more but that he might enter into the darkness of separated humanity and tormented nature and, through his ceaseless prayer, be made by God's grace alone into a means of bringing that grace to bear on the whole tragic circumstances of his time. He was praying and living through the time of the First World War and the rise of Hitler and the beginnings of all that led to the Holocaust. And with all this awareness of pain and sorrow, he was given also a great serenity and peacefulness and goodness about him which profoundly impressed those who knew him.

For all of us in our lesser ways, the Jesus Prayer, as well as bringing us into something of this kind of alternation which St Silouan so strikingly experienced, also leads us on with him into an ever deepening peace. You can understand how those who taught and practised this kind of prayer were first called 'hesychasts': people of *hesychia* or stillness.

'Enclose your thought within the words of the prayer,' said John Climacus, and early on the prayer emerged as a way of attaining a stillness in God that is also a movement into God—so that at the same time we are 'still and still moving'.

That's another way of putting what I was saying earlier. Rejoicing at being at home—and yet still travelling. Being here—and yet being there more fully. It has already grasped you—yet you are reaching out to grasp more. It's that whole understanding of the Christian life which is so very Pauline. There is a peace which lies beyond all our striving to which we are brought as the prayer becomes more and more of a river, a stream running through our consciousness. And it transcends our alternations at length in the One who alone, through the cross and resurrection of Christ, holds together the now and the not yet. The Jesus Prayer constantly enables us to be drawn into that still centre.

It's very much the same thing that Bishop Stephen Verney used to say to us when he was taking a Bible study with a group of us long ago. We would all sit round discussing the passage. Perhaps it would be the Gospel of John, which he was particularly gifted at studying. Or perhaps a passage from one of the Pauline epistles. Then, after we had all shared our thoughts of varied value and it was coming to a close, Stephen Verney would say, 'Right now! Put the books away and just take a phrase that has come from the passage.' Often one or two people would suggest a phrase. Perhaps we would take 'rooted and grounded in love', or, 'that we should be to the praise of his glory', or that we are 'accepted in the beloved'. But we would take the phrase, wherever it was from, and just let it sink down into our hearts. Perhaps for a quarter of an hour we would just sit quietly, dwelling on that particular phrase.

I think that is something which it is quite right to do, and it is a concentration of all the other things that we are doing and feeling and thinking, transcending them, and going beyond them.

So to pray the Jesus Prayer doesn't mean that you

are not having all kinds of conversations and reading and exploring and doing various other things, and praying discursively as well as praying the Jesus Prayer. It doesn't exclude meditative prayer of a different kind.

I found the most interesting combination of those two ways of praying when I went to St Beuno's on an eight-day retreat. We were using Ignatius' own meditations and the Ignatian method, in which you focus on a particular scene in the Gospels. You enter into the scene, and you see yourself and imagine yourself as one of the different people. Then, while you are in that situation, you imagine Jesus approaching you and speaking to you. And as that happened each time I found myself moving into the Jesus Prayer and through the steady beat of the prayer, being given a fresh realization not only of the presence of Jesus Christ, but also through that presence a discernment of the will of God for me at that time and through that Gospel scene.

In praying the prayer there do come times when you want to rest in complete silence. Those who use the prayer cord sometimes when they come to the wooden bead do not use it as I mentioned above for intercession but instead just simply rest upon it for a while like a bird resting on the warm upcurrents of the wind, supported and held by them. That's just an image, but if the prayer is like the wing-beats then at a certain point you just glide—and then start beating again with the wings. It's a moment of pause—and sometimes at that point I combine it with a kind of dialogue expressing things that are in my mind. Then when I have done that for a bit I go back to the Jesus Prayer.

It is rather like what I did on my retreat at St

Beuno's, when I left the Ignatian meditation and moved into the Jesus Prayer. I found that helpful, and I find this helpful. I pause in the Jesus Prayer, and talk with God for a little while. And I can then return. It is perfectly combined in such a way, and I found those beads reminded me of that.

The stillness is good after the beating of the wings, and I find it helpful just to have a moment of total silence and then to launch very gently into the prayer again. A very slight pause—and then on to the next prayer.

10

Using the Jesus Prayer in a group

It is quite possible to use the Jesus Prayer in a group, and I have done this here in Coventry. I have done so very tentatively, because I felt that people might feel imprisoned. I thought that they might not want to hear a voice which kept on repeating the prayer. But then I thought, 'Well, I and many other people have been to the monastery and have found it helpful. So why should I think that other people won't?'

I have deanery groups here in the chapel, and people come from all the different parishes. What I do at the groups is to talk about silent prayer, because this is the approach which I have found more helpful than any other. I tell them that I have found the idea of this repeated prayer very helpful, and on several occasions I have started saying the Jesus Prayer aloud just as we did in the monastery.

The last time I did it the people who were there all said to me afterwards, 'That was wonderful!' And I have done it with our Bishop's Council, the Standing Committee of the Diocesan Synod.

The Bishop's Council felt that as we were calling the diocese to prayer, we should pray together ourselves. Afterwards several people said to me, to my amazement, 'That is one of the most important moments that we have experienced.' So I realized what a tremendous power it had. And that has emboldened me.

I need plenty of emboldening sometimes with something like this—to start not only teaching about it but also leading groups in it. And getting others to lead it.

Just as I was thrilled to lead the Jesus Prayer in an ecumenical group, so other people can do it. It's a very good corporate exercise. What I did was to use the cord, so I said the prayer a hundred times. What you don't want is to have to think about it at the time. So if anyone was going to use the prayer in this way it would be helpful to get hold of a cord. You pray it a hundred times (and have the three pauses) and then you stop.

What I feel happens in this prayer is that you don't make images or even think thoughts. You draw your mind away from the thoughts and images, because this kind of prayer is a transcending prayer. You draw your mind away from the very things that might preoccupy you. But you don't do that unkindly. Just gently. Draw it back from the other distractions; and from falling asleep; and from all the things that we do all the time.

And we mustn't be horrified by the things that we find ourselves doing—by all the fantasies and dreams and stray thoughts that float in. We just bring our mind back. And the prayer is very well designed for that. You are repeating the actual name, 'Lord Jesus Christ'. And even if you suddenly realize that you have lost your concentration you can at once come back again, and the mention of that name is again the invocation of the presence.

When you are praying the prayer yourself you can actually repeat the words without thinking. If each time you invoke the name you keep gently drawing yourself back to the presence, to wanting to want to be in the presence of God, that will happen. Then you focus on simply the presence and the love of God and you don't think about anything else, any disposition, even any act of prayer. It's a practice of the presence of God and it's a being in that presence, relaxed and alert.

As you go on praying that presence comes to be a presence within you, around you, over you, and in all things. And so gradually the sense of the presence grows. And however sharply and strongly you are distracted you don't worry about it, and you don't reproach yourself. His love is here. So you just draw back into the presence.

He is coming to meet us. He has already grasped us. So that sense of joy and thanksgiving should be a very strong sense. That must be the predominant sense.

For me the prayer has always ended with the words, 'Lord Jesus Christ, Son of God'—not with 'have mercy on me'. He is enough. He is all.

It is so important to discover that love. It is a love unknown. We still don't reach out for it—we don't know anything like enough of being loved and of God's love holding us. And holding all those for whom we pray.

So this aspect of the prayer is that sense of being loved, that sense of home-coming, the sense that there is no condemnation—of being utterly accepted and being drawn into an intimate relationship. It is only within the security of that love and that embrace that we begin to want to say, 'I am sorry.' And we also want to say, 'I love you—and I would love to be very different yet to be more fully myself.'

So we begin to desire the transformation of the inner being—and a transformation of all those for

83

whom we pray—and a transformation of the whole world.

And therefore the prayer springs out of this deep confidence in being loved and accepted, and in recollecting we recollect our real self. That is what we are praying for. Asking to become more and more ourself and to lose the false little ego which is distracting us and undermining us.

We are asking that we might be enabled to find ourselves. To do what we were made to do—to find our true self in communion with God. To be what we were made to be and (whatever has gone wrong in the past) still can be, which is so wonderful. That is what 'have mercy on me' is about. It is saying, 'Help me to be. Enfold me in your redemptive and creative love.'

The Germans have a phrase, *'erbarme dich unser'*, which means 'mercify us', and I like that. It is about the mercy which is positively holding us. The mercy which is lovingkindness. 'I desire mercy and not sacrifice... I desire lovingkindness.'

We ourselves look to his mercy, his compassion and his lovingkindness. 'Have compassion on me. Mercify me. Grasp me in your lovingkindness. Enfold me in your love.'

So that is the nature of the yearning: 'Have mercy.' And as he 'mercifies us' he is leading us into a yearning to be transformed ourselves and also a yearning for the transformation of all things.

All the time this yearning is taking place within the love that is saying, 'Yes! I am making new. I have made it new. And I will make it new.' That is the great promise of God.

So the second part of the prayer, 'have mercy on me' is something that we don't think about at the

LORD JESUS CHRIST HAVE MERCY ON ME

time. We aren't thinking about its meaning. We are repeating the prayer and just focusing on the presence. But the presence is transforming us. The presence is that through which our tears and our cries and our sighs and our groaning are brought into God's purpose and even used in the fulfilment of things.

So there are these dual strains in the prayer. They are present in all prayer and in all worship and in all of Christian life. And they are present in this repeated prayer. All those things are there in the practice of the presence which is what the Jesus Prayer is.

It is enough to repeat the prayer in the love of the presence, just wanting to want to love. And the resting, the rejoicing and the yearning needn't be expressed in words or even in thoughts. They are just implicit in the words of the prayer, as you repeat them gently, looking to Christ:

> Lord Jesus Christ, Son of God, have mercy
> on me.

Some forms of the prayer and some of the prayers of the prayer, (like Sophrony himself), have added the words 'a sinner' at the end when they are praying it on their own, not corporately. One might think that those words emphasize too much what our whole culture and tradition has so battered us with. And we want really to break away from the burdensomeness and the false guilt that they have laid upon us.

Yet I can understand why they added the words. If you appear to yourself to be nothing more than a sinner, a sinful human being, a child crying in the night, then forgiveness is the way to break through to everything that you really have in yourself. It is the way for all of us, aware of our weakness. Aware, perhaps, of the truth of Richard Baxter's words: that he preached 'as one who may never preach again, as a dying man to dying men'.

Some prefer to drop those words 'a sinner' from the prayer, because of their association with that false guilt the Christian Church has sometimes imposed on us.

But some people would want to pray the full prayer, 'have mercy on me, a sinner'. Just reminding us of the reality that it is this sinful world, and my sinful being, which is being transformed. It has been, is being, and will be transformed utterly.

> In this the love of God was made manifest
> among us, that God sent his only Son into
> the world, so that we might live through
> him. In this is love, not that we loved God
> but that he loved us and sent his Son to be
> the expiation for our sins.
>
> 1 John 4:9–10 (RSV)

So as we come to draw it together the third thing to be aware of about the Jesus Prayer is the way in which in Christ, and in our union with him, two facets of our awareness of God are combined. On the one side, the joy, the beauty, the goodness, the sense of restoration and the sheer wonder and ecstasy of God are held together with, on the other side, all the despair, all the horror, all the frustration, all the bitterness, darkness and sadness of our experience of life which can seem so utterly disappointing, disillusioning and disintegrating.

It is these two facets that are being held completely together on the cross and in the risen, wounded Christ. Held together in heaven as well as on earth.

We look to heaven, and at Christ—already in heaven—making intercession for us. From there we are sent back, as it were, to the wounds of this world. There is no escaping. It is these very wounds that are being caught up into heaven.

It is rather like Karl Barth's wonderful description of Mozart, in which he says that he hears the joy of the whole universe. Within it he hears the light, yet within that the shadow and the tragedy. The whole contains the two.

It is this truth that great works of art and great moments of faith bring home to us—the awareness that even through the horror and the tragedy the light still shines, and that the darkness never extinguishes it. In the end the light enfolds and will draw the horror and the tragedy in. We cannot see how. It is naked faith. We see that—yet we do not see—but it is being held.

Therefore the Jesus Prayer is a prayer of the most utter realism—and yet a prayer of the most total confidence in God's love and in the joy and completeness of everything. This holding together comes gradually as we pray this prayer.

The awareness of it will vary enormously depending on what is happening in our own life and in our consciousness of life. The prayer will steady us, and we shall find ourselves held in the knowledge that we are truly sharing in both the power of his resurrection and the fellowship of his suffering.

As we go on praying the prayer we shall become increasingly aware of this, and that we are at the same time both at home in the joy and fulfilment of

God and yet also journeying towards that fulfilment through great difficulty and burdened through frustration.

We find this poise again and again in the New Testament. It is there in the way that St Paul seems to win through to an incredible richness and depth in those wonderful final verses of Romans 8. We really are conscious of being more than conquerors through him that loved us—in spite of the fact that we are as sheep for the slaughter. There is the wonderful paradox.

This is the paradox of the gospel itself. And as we pray, and continue with the prayer, 'Lord Jesus Christ, Son of God, have mercy on me' we are aware of being drawn into the rhythm of the whole universe—a universe which seems to be disintegrating, only to be remade. We are drawn into that, and also into the perfect presence of God. We are aware of (in the words of the famous last line of Dante's *Paradiso*) 'the love that sways the universe'—our own galaxy—'and the other stars'—and of the healing and wholeness for which the universe is made, for which it is destined, and towards which it is being drawn.

That was something which was so lovely in the prayer itself in that monastery. That as we prayed we had a sense of moving together—like a flock of birds—moving in the movement of God himself through the universe. God moving through human lives, through all the imperfection, and through all the fragmentations towards wholeness and healing.

The Jesus Prayer is a participation in that movement of the redemptive love flowing through all things. I believe that the prayer draws us very near to the heart of the universal gospel. I think that is why it has gained such strength in East and West, and why so many people find it a way of being held by that to which they are still reaching out.

Lord Jesus Christ

Son of God

Have mercy on me

Bibliography

The most outstanding and easily accessible book is Kallistos Ware, *The Power of the Name: The Jesus Prayer in Orthodox Spirituality*, Marshall Pickering, 1989 and The Sisters of the Love of God, Convent of the Incarnation, Fairacres, Oxford, 1986.

A good practical book is Brother Ramon, SSF, *Praying the Jesus Prayer: A contemporary introduction to an ancient method of contemplative prayer*, Marshall Pickering, 1988.

A rather more idiosyncratic, but attractive, book is Archimandrite Lev Gillet's book, *On The Invocation of The Name of Jesus by a Monk of the Eastern Church*, published by The Fellowship of St Alban and St Sergius, 52 Ladbroke Grove.

Also by Archimandrite Lev Gillet is *The Jesus Prayer*, revised with a foreword by Kallistos Ware, St Vladimir's Seminary Press, New York, 1987.

The famous little book *The Way of a Pilgrim* translated from the Russian by the Reverend R.M. French, first published in 1930 by Philip Allan, has been republished by SPCK, most recently in a paperback edition in 1973, and has since been reprinted a number of times.

The less valuable, but still interesting, sequel *The Pilgrim Continues His Way* was published by SPCK in a Triangle edition in 1986.

A good little Protestant book on the Jesus Prayer is *The Jesus Prayer: learning to pray from heart*, by a Lutheran author Pere-Olof Sjogren, Triangle, 1986.

Archimandrite Sophrony has written on the Jesus Prayer in *His Life is Mine*, A.R. Mowbray, 1977. He has also written about St Silouan: The Monk of Mount Athos, St Vladimir's Seminary Press, 1973 and Wisdom from Mount Athos, St Vladimir's Seminary Press, 1975.

Another attractive book by a Russian Orthodox author of the nineteenth century is Bishop Ignatius Brianchaninov, *On the Prayer of Jesus*, translated by Father Lazarus, Element Books, Shaftesbury, Dorset, 1987.

Two attractive books which now are out of print, but obtainable from a library are:

Tito Colliander, *The Way of the Ascetics*. The author was a Russian Orthodox layman who lived most of his life in Helsinki, Finland.

Alphonse and Rachel Goettmann, *Prayer of Jesus—Prayer of the Heart*, translated by Theodore and Rebecca Nottingham, Paulist Press, New York, 1991. This is a most attractive book of great power.

Finally, for delving more deeply into the history of the Jesus Prayer, there is Irenee Hausherr, *The Name of Jesus*, translated by Charles Cummings, Cistercian Publications, Kalamazoo, Michigan, 1978.

If you have enjoyed reading *The Jesus Prayer*, you may wish to know that The Bible Reading Fellowship publishes two regular series of Bible reading notes, *New Daylight* and *Guidelines*, which are published three times a year (in January, May and September). *New Daylight* contains printed Bible passages, brief comments and prayers. *Guidelines* contains thought and commentary on the Bible arranged in weekly sections. *New Daylight* is also available in a large print version.

Copies of *New Daylight* and *Guidelines* may be obtained from your local Christian bookshop or by subscription direct from BRF.

A free sample copy of *New Daylight* or *Guidelines* may be obtained by sending an A5 SAE with 38p stamp marked '*New Daylight*' or '*Guidelines*' to BRF. For more information about the full range of BRF publications, write to: The Bible Reading Fellowship, Peter's Way, Sandy Lane West, Oxford OX4 5HG (Tel. 01865 748227).